AF270384

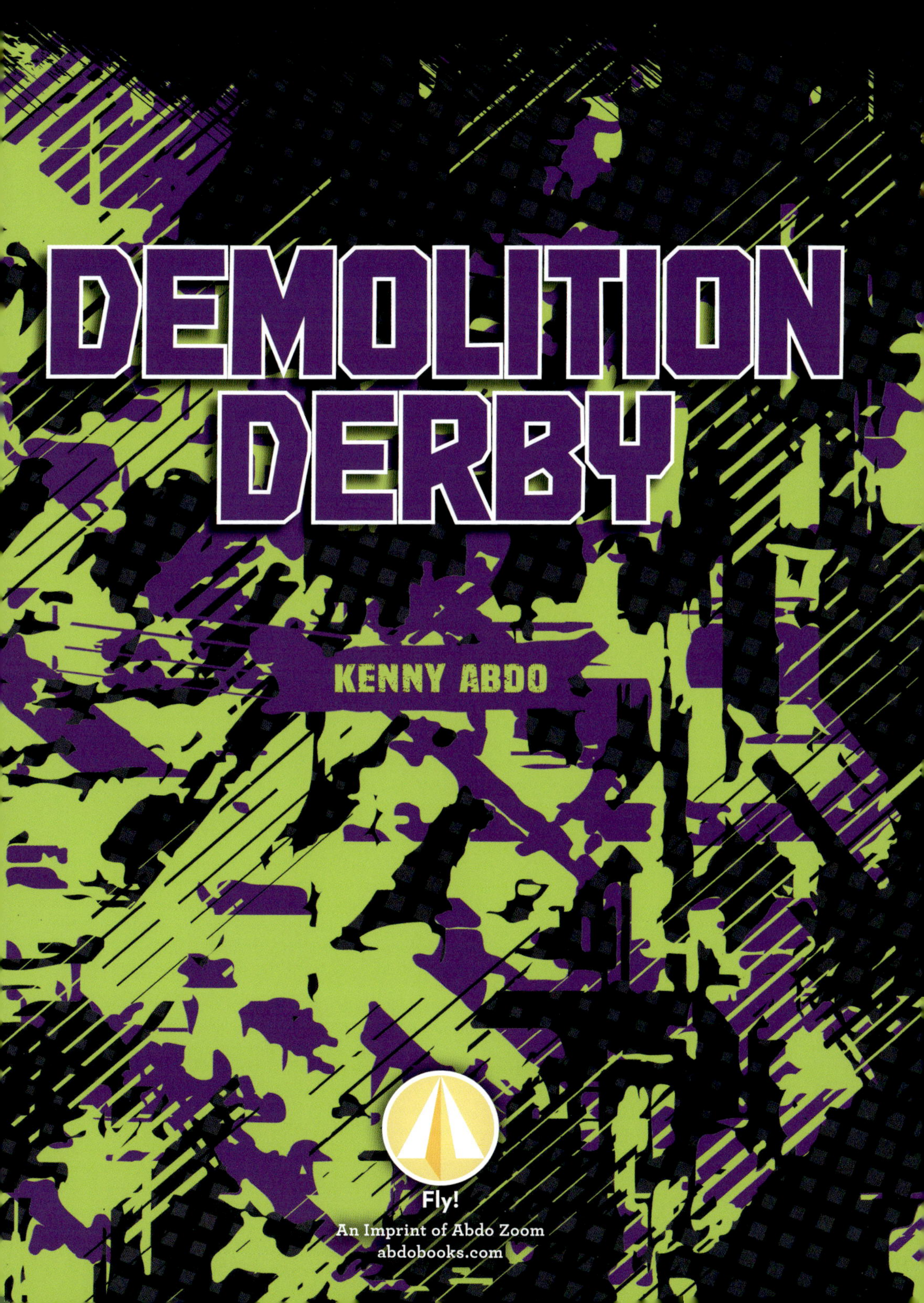

MOTOR MAYHEM
DEMOLITION DERBY
KENNY ABDO
Fly!
An Imprint of Abdo Zoom
abdobooks.com

abdobooks.com

Published by Abdo Zoom, a division of ABDO, P.O. Box 398166, Minneapolis, Minnesota 55439. Copyright © 2024 by Abdo Consulting Group, Inc. International copyrights reserved in all countries. No part of this book may be reproduced in any form without written permission from the publisher. Fly!™ is a trademark and logo of Abdo Zoom.

Printed in the United States of America, North Mankato, Minnesota.
052023
092023

Photo Credits: Alamy, AP Images, Getty Images, Flickr, Shutterstock, ©AllieKF p.10/ CC BY-NC-SA 2.0, ©Terry Evans, B.A.T. p16
Production Contributors: Kenny Abdo, Jennie Forsberg, Grace Hansen
Design Contributors: Candice Keimig, Neil Klinepier

Library of Congress Control Number: 2022946927

Publisher's Cataloging-in-Publication Data

Names: Abdo, Kenny, author.
Title: Demolition derby / by Kenny Abdo
Description: Minneapolis, Minnesota : Abdo Zoom, 2024 | Series: Motor mayhem |
    Includes online resources and index.
Identifiers: ISBN 9781098281427 (lib. bdg.) | ISBN 9781098282127 (ebook) |
    ISBN 9781098282479 (Read-to-me ebook)
Subjects: LCSH: Automobiles, Racing--Juvenile literature. | Vehicles--Juvenile
    literature. | Demolition derbies--Juvenile literature.
Classification: DDC 796.72--dc23

TABLE OF CONTENTS

Demolition Derby 4

Start Your Engines 8

Mayhem 12

Burnout 20

Glossary 22

Online Resources 23

Index 24

DEMOLITION DERBY

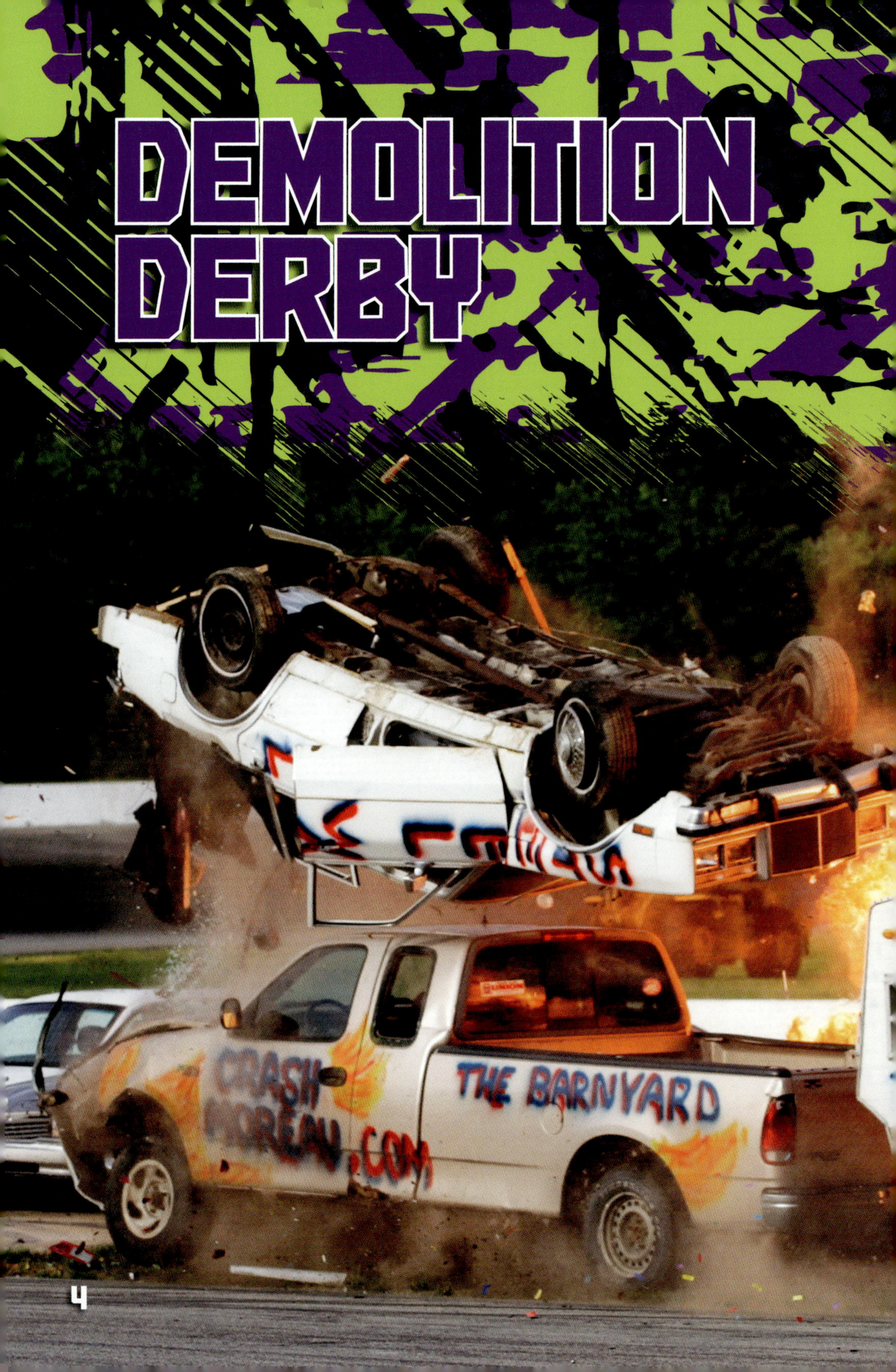

From broken bumpers to explosive thrill shows, demolition derbies smash every fan's expectations!

Crashing through North America to the United Kingdom and Australia, audiences cannot get enough of the thrilling destruction!

FLATROCK
F

START YOUR ENGINES

Some believe that demolition derbies began in the 1930s. However, reports say that **stock car** racer Larry Mendelsohn kick-started the craze in 1958!

Derbies became trendy at fairs around the US. The **motorsport** grew in popularity after being televised around the country. But nothing beat seeing the mayhem live!

STARSHIP
2000
GEMINI

MAYHEM

A demolition derby is a competition involving **scrap cars**. Drivers will **soup up** their vehicles with cages on the inside and **roll bars**.

The event starts with the cars in a circle on a dirt field or **track**.

The drivers then smash into their rivals until only one vehicle is left working.

Some derbies have different rules. Drivers must wear helmets and eye protection at all times. The driver who puts on the most exciting performance receives a "Mad Dog" trophy.

WINTER SLHM
TRUCKS
MADDOG
St. Paul, MN "19"
dog 8.17
slam
r Mn.
RON

There are many types of demolition derbies. Some cars are destroyed using the trucks at Monster Truck Rallies. Minivan Demolition Derbies have also become popular.

PIECES D'AUTO
DAUDELIN
50
RADIO LASALLE
FM 100,1
WWW.REMORQUAGEMENARD.COM
GARAGE MARTIN
514-8
95
514-820-7
135
00
WWW.ISADIRECT.CA

BURNOUT
75
20

Today, events are still held throughout the world. From **county fairs** to giant arenas, demolition derbies crush all other **motorsports**!

county fair – a yearly fair held at a set location in a county that includes local farming products, games, and rides.

motorsport – a sport involving the racing of motor vehicles, like cars and motorcycles.

roll bar – an overhead metal bar in a car that is designed to protect the driver in case of a rollover.

scrap car – a broken or beaten-up car that has no resale value.

soup up – to upgrade the power, body, or performance of something, like a car.

stock car – a normal car that has been customized for racing.

track – a course laid out for racing, usually made of dirt.

ONLINE RESOURCES

Booklinks
NONFICTION NETWORK
FREE! ONLINE NONFICTION RESOURCES

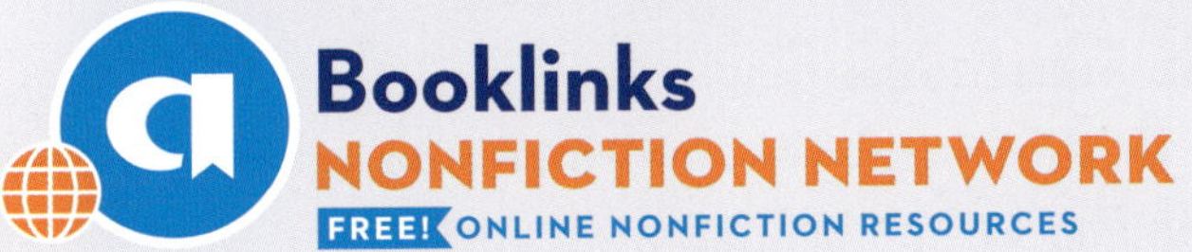

To learn more about demolition derbies, please visit **abdobooklinks.com** or scan this QR code. These links are routinely monitored and updated to provide the most current information available.

INDEX

Australia 6

awards 16

cars 13, 14, 15, 18

drivers 13, 15, 16

events 10, 14, 21

Mendelsohn, Larry 9

Minivan Demolition Derby 18

Monster Trucks 18

North America 6

origin 9

United Kingdom 6